ABC

Bible Verses for Little Ones

Rebecca Lutzer

Illustrated by
Mary Eakin

HARVEST kids

HARVEST HOUSE PUBLISHERS
EUGENE, OREGON

Cover and interior design by Mary Eakin

ABC Bible Verses for Little Ones

Published by Harvest House Publishers
Eugene, Oregon 97408
www.harvesthousepublishers.com
ISBN 978-0-7369-7343-4 (hardcover)

Library of Congress Cataloging-in-Publication Data

Names: Lutzer, Rebecca, author.
Title: ABC Bible verses for little ones / Rebecca Lutzer ; illustrated by Mary Eakin.
Description: Eugene : Harvest House Publishers, 2018.
Identifiers: LCCN 2018012577 (print) | LCCN 2018020748 (ebook) | ISBN 9780736973441 (ebook) | ISBN 9780736973434 (hardcover)
Subjects: LCSH: Bible—Children's use. | Bible—Memorizing—Juvenile literature. | Bible—Quotations—Juvenile literature.
Classification: LCC BS618 (ebook) | LCC BS618 .L879 2018 (print) | DDC 220.95/05—dc23
LC record available at https://lccn.loc.gov/2018012577

Printed in China

19 20 21 22 23 24 25 26 27 / LP / 10 9 8 7 6 5 4 3 2

Lovingly dedicated to the
memory of our first grandchild,
Sarah Bourne. Though she never had the
opportunity to live and grow up in the grace
and knowledge of the Lord, she has been safe
in the arms of Jesus these past 22 years. May
this book guide other little ones to know the
wonder of Jesus's love and salvation.

Angel

In heaven their angels always see the face of my Father.
MATTHEW 18:10 ESV

Believe

Believe in the Lord Jesus.

ACTS 16:31

Children

Let the little children come to me.

MATTHEW 19:14

Discipline

God disciplines us for our good.

HEBREWS 12:10

Eye

Open my eyes that I may see
wonderful things in your law.
PSALM 119:18

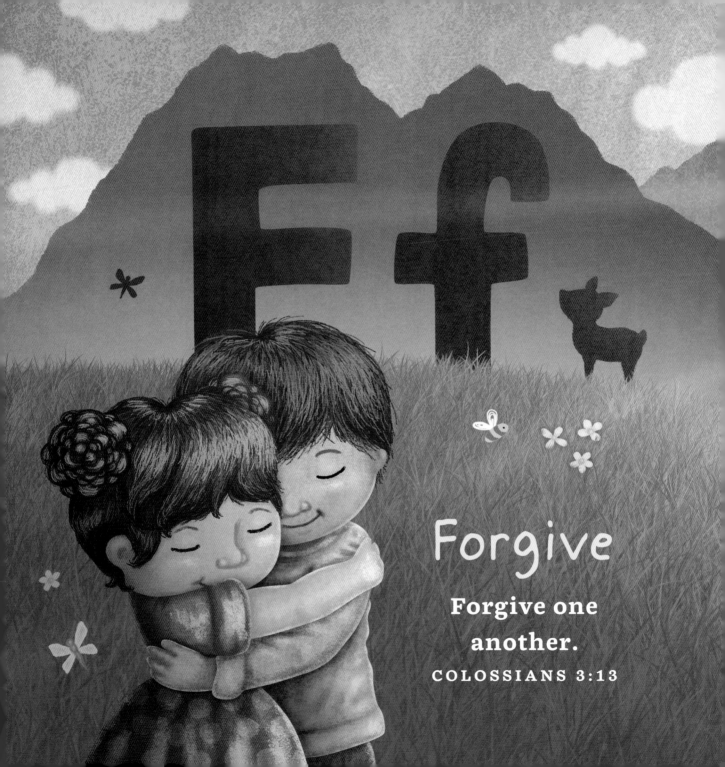

Forgive

Forgive one another.
COLOSSIANS 3:13

Gg

God

God is great.

JOB 36:26 NKJV

Heart

I have hidden
your word in
my heart.
PSALM 119:11

I am happy to
do your will,
O my God.

PSALM 40:8 GW

Jesus

Name him Jesus, for he
will save his people from
their sins.

MATTHEW 1:21 NLT

Kk

Kind

Be kind to each other.

EPHESIANS 4:32 NLT

The Lord is good and his love endures forever.

PSALM 100:5

Love

Lord, You are God,
who made heaven
and earth.

ACTS 4:24 NKJV

Mm

Made

Name

**Those who know
your name trust you,
O Lord.**

PSALM 9:10 GW

Obey

Children, obey
your parents.

EPHESIANS 6:1

Quick

Be quick to listen.

JAMES 1:19

Qq

Rejoice

Rejoice and be glad.
PSALM 118:24 NKJV

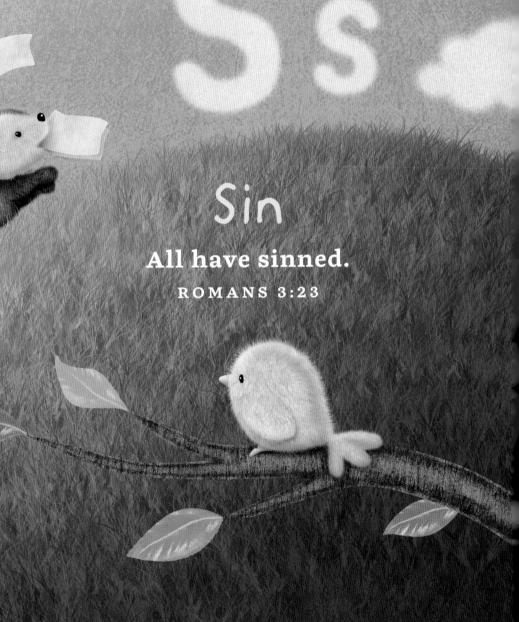

Ss

Sin

All have sinned.

ROMANS 3:23

Trust

Trust in the LORD.

PROVERBS 3:5

Uu

Us

**The LORD is God!
He made us, and we
are his.**

PSALM 100:3 NLT

Value

Godliness is of value in every way.

1 TIMOTHY 4:8 ESV

Word

**The word of God is alive
and active.**

HEBREWS 4:12

Exalt

Exalt the LORD our God.

PSALM 99:5

Yy

Youth

**Since my youth, God,
you have taught me.**

PSALM 71:17

Zion

Those who trust in the LORD are like Mount Zion, which cannot be shaken.

PSALM 125:1

Dear Little One,

The words in this book come from
a very special book called the Bible.
The Bible tells us who God is and
who we are. We learn about the world
God made. God wants us to know Him,
and love Him, and obey His words.
God loves you very much. You are
precious to Him.

From my heart to yours,

"Grandma" Rebecca